2/10

MODERN ROLE MODELS

Adam Sandler

Michael V. Uschan

Mason Crest Publishers

Produced by OTTN Publishing in association with
21st Century Publishing and Communications, Inc.

MASON CREST PUBLISHERS INC.
370 Reed Road
Broomall, Pennsylvania 19008
(866) MCP-BOOK (toll free)
www.masoncrest.com

Printed in the United States of America.

First Printing

9 8 7 6 5 4 3 2 1

Library of Congress Cataloging-in-Publication Data

Uschan, Michael V., 1948–
    Adam Sandler / by Michael V. Uschan.
      p. cm. — (Modern role models)
    Includes bibliographical references and index.
    ISBN-13: 978-1-4222-0507-5 (hardcover) — ISBN-13: 978-1-4222-0794-9 (pbk.)
    1. Sandler, Adam—Juvenile literature. 2. Actors—United States—Biography—
Juvenile literature. I. Title.
    PN2287.S275U83 2008
    792.02'8092—dc22
    [B]   2008020429

CROSS-CURRENTS

*In the ebb and flow of the currents of life we are each influenced
by many people, places, and events that we directly experience
or have learned about. Throughout the chapters of this book you
will come across CROSS-CURRENTS reference boxes. These
boxes direct you to a CROSS-CURRENTS section in the back
of the book that contains fascinating and informative sidebars
and related pictures. Go on.* ▸▸

CONTENTS

Adam Sandler accepts the award for Favorite Male Movie Star at Nickelodeon's 20th Annual Kids' Choice Awards, held on March 31, 2007, at University of California's Pauley Pavilion, in Los Angeles, California. That same year, the popular comedian was also named Spike TV's Guy's Guy. The Golden Globe-nominated actor is a musician, screenwriter, and film producer as well.

1

A Guy's Guy

IN 2007 ADAM SANDLER SHOWED WHY HE IS ONE of the world's most beloved film stars. Adam starred in the hit movies *I Now Pronounce You Chuck and Larry* and *Reign Over Me*. He also won two honors— "Favorite Male Movie Star" in the Nickelodeon Kids' Choice Awards and "Ultimate Guy's Guy" in the first Spike TV Guys' Choice awards.

⇒ A SUCCESSFUL "MORON" ⇐

Adam first vaulted to stardom in 1995 with the film *Billy Madison*. In that movie, Adam plays the title character, Billy Madison, a spoiled young rich man who does nothing but hang out with his friends and spend his dad's money. His father, played by Darren McGavin, decides that Billy needs to learn responsibility. He orders him to go back to school and repeat every grade from kindergarten through high school in 24 weeks. If Billy does not pass, he will never get any more money from his family. The funny parts of the movie come from watching a grown man attend school with little kids and teenagers. He even falls in love with his third-grade teacher. Along with the laughs, Madison satisfies his dad, wins his true love, and becomes a better person.

Billy Madison established Adam's trademark character—the lovable loser who seems doomed to defeat but manages to overcome his problems. Adam has continued to be immensely successful and popular since his first starring role in that movie because he is able to make people laugh like few other entertainers can. Adam's humor is whimsical and offbeat. Some movie reviewers have criticized his style of humor because it is childishly silly. They mockingly label him the "goofball king" and even a "moron." But Adam does not care what critics call him as long as he can make people laugh. In an interview with a British magazine, Adam jokingly claimed that

> **"I've been called a moron since I was about four. My father called me a moron. My grandfather said I was a moron. And a lot of times when I'm driving, I hear I'm a moron. I like being a moron."**

Adam does not mind being considered a moron because he is so successful. His wacky humor has helped him make as much as $25 million for one movie. When *I Now Pronounce You Chuck and Larry* opened on March 23, 2007, fans of his unique brand of humor bought $34.2 million in tickets in just one weekend. That was enough to edge *Harry Potter and the Order of the Phoenix* out of first place in U.S. ticket sales for that period. In the movie, Adam and Kevin James play two straight Brooklyn firefighters who pretend to get married even though they are not gay. The mock marriage is designed to help Kevin's character retain his life insurance benefits for his children. The hilarious film is full of the wild stunts and crazy dialogue that have made Adam a star.

CROSS-CURRENTS

To learn how Adam and Kevin James became good friends while working on their movie, read "Buddies in Real Life." Go to page 48. ▶▶

In his other big 2007 movie, Adam proved he can be a powerful dramatic actor. In *Reign Over Me* Adam plays Charlie Fineman, a survivor of the September 11, 2001, terrorist attacks against the United States. Fineman acts likes

Kevin James (left) and Adam Sandler attend the 2007 Los Angeles, California, premiere of *I Now Pronounce You Chuck and Larry*. Like Adam, Kevin got his start doing stand-up comedy. In the late 1990s he landed a role on the sitcom *Everyone Loves Raymond* and soon afterward starred in his own show, *The King of Queens*.

A movie poster from the 2007 film *Reign Over Me.* **Many critics raved about Adam Sandler's performance in the drama, in which he played a character unable to deal with effects of a terrible tragedy. Although Adam became famous through his comedic roles, he has shown talent in several films as a dramatic actor.**

he is crazy because he cannot bear to remember the death of his family on that tragic day. In the movie, a friend played by Don Cheadle helps him cope with the devastating loss of his loved ones. Adam was universally praised for his superb performance. Movie critic William Arnold writes:

> **"The most heavily dramatic Sandler vehicle to date is a striking, genuinely touching, meticulously well-acted friendship parable, and a big audience pleaser. He stays clear of his usual repertoire of cutesy tricks, his more explosive moments have a frightening intensity and, in one or two of his scenes, he's authentically heartbreaking."**

A MULTITALENTED STAR

Adam Sandler is more than just a talented actor, however. He started entertaining people in the 1980s as a **stand-up comedian** when he was only a teenager. Adam then began working in television. His big break came in 1990, when he was hired for *Saturday Night Live (SNL)*. After a year writing jokes and skits for other actors, Adam became one of the show's most popular performers.

His *SNL* success led to Adam making five comedy albums, which have sold millions of copies. He began getting small roles in movies and became a star with his performances in *Billy Madison* and in *Happy Gilmore* (1996). Adam also became a movie **producer**. He started a company called Happy Madison Productions—the name combines the titles of his first two hit movies—so he could create his own films instead of just acting in them. The company has produced several of Adam's biggest hits, including *Big Daddy* and *The Wedding Singer*. Adam has also helped write the **scripts** for many of his movies. Adam has found professional success as a talented actor, comedian, film producer, and writer.

Adam Sandler was born into a Jewish working-class family in the New York City borough of Brooklyn. However, he spent most of his childhood in the small community of Manchester, New Hampshire. He is the third of four children, with one brother, Scott, and two sisters, Elizabeth and Valerie.

2

Growing up Happy

IN HIS 1998 HIT COMEDY *THE WATERBOY*, ADAM Sandler plays Bobby Boucher, a weird young man from Louisiana who was raised alone by an even stranger mother. Adam's own childhood was the exact opposite of that of his funny movie character. He grew up in Manchester, New Hampshire, in a family that was loving and normal.

⟫ STAN AND JUDY'S KID ⟪

Adam Richard Sandler was born on September 9, 1966, in Brooklyn, New York. His mother, Judy, was a nursery-school teacher, and his father, Stanley, worked as an electrical engineer. When Adam was five years old, his family moved to Manchester, a small community of about 100,000 people. In addition to being the home of one of the world's funniest comedians, Manchester is also home to members of the famed rock band Aerosmith—one of Adam's favorite groups.

Adam was the youngest of four children—he has a brother, Scott, and sisters Elizabeth and Valerie. Stanley and Judy Sandler lavished love on their kids and encouraged them to do things that they wanted to do. For Adam, that meant performing. When Adam was only seven years old, he began singing songs like "The Candy Man" at a local nursing home to entertain patients. Adam also liked making his family laugh by telling jokes and even imitating the way his father sneezed. Stanley Sandler loved classic comedians like the Marx Brothers and Jerry Lewis. He and Adam watched them on television, and their zany antics helped inspire Adam's own efforts to make people laugh.

CROSS-CURRENTS

For Adam's thoughts on how his parents influenced him when he was growing up, read "A Loving Family." Go to page 49. ▶▶

When Adam entered Manchester Central High School in 1980, he began to develop the comic talents that would one day make him a star. He became a class clown who would do anything to get a laugh. Robert Schiavone was the high school's guidance counselor. In an interview with the *Florida Times Union* newspaper, Schiavone recalled that Adam's teachers did not always appreciate his attempts at humor:

> **❝He used our school, the cafeteria, the courtyard and the classrooms to perform. We were all his audience. The difference, though, was that some-times his humor would get him in trouble instead of make him money.❞**

Adam was punished several times for interrupting classes with stunts like tossing a head of lettuce out of a classroom window or imitating fellow students or teachers. The punishment was sometimes "internal suspension," which meant he had to stay in a detention hall all day instead of attending class. Adam showed up for one detention carrying a pillow and television and watched his favorite shows. The school had to change the rules to stop students from repeating his trick. Detention was supposed to be punishment, not fun!

≫ THE YOUNG ENTERTAINER ≪

Adam graduated from high school in 1984. That summer he took his first step on the road from class clown to professional comedian when he visited his brother, Scott, who was a law student at Boston University. The brothers went to Stitches, a comedy club that allowed anyone to perform. Scott knew his brother was funny and urged him to tell some jokes. Even though he was only 17, Adam nervously walked onto

The Marx Brothers (from left to right, front row): Chico and Harpo; (back row) Zeppo and Groucho. The comedian brothers transferred their popular stage comedy of the 1910s to film during the 1920s through the 1940s. Among their best-known movies are *Duck Soup* **(1933) and** *A Night at the Opera* **(1935).**

CROSS-CURRENTS

To learn about some other talented and successful Jewish comedians who preceded Adam Sandler, read "Jewish Comedians." Go to page 50. ▶▶

the stage. He got a few laughs, and the experience made him want to become a comedian.

In the fall of 1984 Adam began attending New York University (NYU). During his summer vacation, Adam continued performing at comedy clubs, and he kept doing that that while he attended college. Adam admits it was hard to perform in front of live audiences at clubs like the Comic Strip. He once told the *San Francisco Chronicle* newspaper:

> **❝It took a lot of time for me to get comfortable on stage. I would be very nervous. I couldn't concentrate; my thoughts were scattered. I froze in front of audiences a lot of times. What happens as a comedian is your skin gets thick.❞**

What Adam meant by a "thick skin" is that comics have to learn to ignore critical comments from people in the audience. Adam did that. Even more importantly, Adam learned how to make people laugh.

⟫ BREAKING INTO TELEVISION ⟪

As an NYU theater student, Adam was allowed to take classes at the Lee Strasberg Theater Institute, one of the world's most prestigious acting schools. Adam must have learned something, because he was soon acting on television.

After **casting agent** Barry Moss saw Adam's nightclub act, he was so impressed with his talent that he helped Adam get a small part on *The Cosby Show*. The hit comedy starred legendary African American comedian Bill Cosby. Adam played Smitty, a goofy friend of Theo Huxtable, Cosby's son on the series. Adam's first appearance on the show came on December 3, 1987. Adam played Smitty in two **episodes** in 1987 and two more in 1988. He had several memorable scenes with Cosby, who reacted humorously to the quirky character that Adam created.

Adam landed several other television jobs while he was still in college. From 1987 to 1990, Adam appeared on the MTV television trivia game show *Remote Control* as "Trivia Delinquent" or "Stud Boy."

One of Adam's first spots on television was as Theo's friend Smitty on four episodes of *The Cosby Show* during the 1987–1988 season. The popular situation comedy, which ran from 1984 to 1992, centered on the well-off Huxtable family, headed by physician father, Cliff, played by Bill Cosby (center), and his wife, Clair, played by Phylicia Rashad (far left).

He even went on tour with the show when it filmed shows at various college campuses. And in 1990, Adam played a drug dealer in an ABC *Afterschool Special.*

In the summer of 1990, Adam quit New York University so he could move to California. He had learned a lot about performing while studying at NYU. However, his experience performing in comedy clubs and on television would prove to be even more important in paving the way for his rise to stardom.

In 1990 Adam Sandler moved to Los Angeles, California, where he found a ready audience while doing stand-up comedy at the Improv, the city's famous comedy club. Soon Adam's talent for improvisation—performing spontaneously, without a script or other preparation—landed him a job on the late-night television show *Saturday Night Live*.

3

The Multitalented Adam Sandler

ADAM SANDLER ALWAYS WANTED TO BECOME a world-famous entertainer. His nightclub and television work in the late 1980s had brought him a modest measure of success, but Adam knew he had to do something sensational to become a big star. The feat that would help him achieve his goal was to win a spot on *Saturday Night Live*.

➤ ADAM'S BIG BREAK ➤

Adam had been a successful comedian in New York. But he knew that to achieve real fame in comedy, he would have to go to Los Angeles because that is where the nation's most successful young comics were performing. They worked there because they hoped their acts would win them parts in movies and television shows. This would allow them to make more money and become more famous. So, in the summer of 1990, Adam, moved to Los Angeles. (He later went back to New York University, graduating in 1991 with a bachelor of fine arts degree.) Adam lived in an apartment in Los Angeles with two of his college classmates, Jack Giarraputo and Judd Apatow.

Adam quickly became a regular at the Improv, the most famous comedy club in Los Angeles. Barry Moss was Adam's agent during the period in which he played comedy clubs. Some comedians rehearse the jokes they are going to tell over and over and mostly recite their act from memory. But Moss said Adam was different and never prepared any material before going onstage. Instead, Adam liked to do **improvisational** comedy. Adam first wanted to see what his audience was like—whether the people listening were young or old, hip or square. He would then select jokes to fit the type of people he was performing for on that particular night. Comedians are often **heckled** by people in the audience. Adam's ability to improvise jokes helped him come back with rapid-fire responses to taunts from hecklers that would make everyone else in the audience laugh.

The comic genius Adam displayed in the famous club soon came to the attention of Lorne Michaels, the legendary *SNL* creator. Michaels was always looking for new talent for the hit show. He arranged for Adam and Chris Rock, another young comic destined for stardom, to **audition** for the show on the same night. The audition was held in a Chicago nightclub, and the two comics had to perform their stand-up comedy acts.

Both comedians did well enough to win jobs for the 1990–1991 season. Although Adam was hired as a writer, he had a chance to appear briefly in some of the **skits** he and other writers created for the show. Adam was tense the first time he was on camera on December 8, 1990, because he said some lines with famous actor Tom Hanks:

> **"I** remember telling Hanks right before, 'Hoo, I'm nervous.' And he goes, 'Hey it's going to be all right.' I said, 'Man, I feel like I'm going to faint or something.' He goes, 'Well don't.'**"**

Adam did not faint. He also did well enough with his writing and in his brief acting stints during that first season that he was hired as

Adam was hired as a writer by Lorne Michaels, the creator and producer of the edgy, topical NBC show *Saturday Night Live*. Except for a brief break in the early 1980s, Michaels has run the show since its first broadcast in 1975. By 1991 Adam had moved up from *SNL* writer to a full-time cast member.

a regular cast member for the following season. It would not be long before Adam would become one of the show's biggest stars.

⋙ A SATURDAY NIGHT LIVE STAR ⋘

Michaels hired Adam because his comedy act had shown the television producer how inventive and original the young comic's humor was. Adam continued creating characters for himself that became

CROSS-CURRENTS

To learn how SNL has helped launch the careers of other young comedians, read "The Power of Saturday Night Live." Go to page 51. ▶▶

favorites of millions of people who watched the 90-minute show every Saturday night.

One of Adam's funniest characters was Cajun Man, who answered questions in one or two-words that always ended with the suffix *-tion* or a similar sound. In 1992 Adam told the *Times-Picayune* newspaper of New Orleans that he got the idea for Cajun Man while eating with friends in a restaurant:

❝It's just a stupid thing. We were sitting in this restaurant and this guy next us was talking real loud and he kept hitting his 'yions' real hard, and every time he said something like 'reserva-SHEEYOHN' we would laugh really hard. We laughed all night. So when we were driving around later that night, every-thing I said was like that. We saw a sign that said 'Hil-TOHN' and we saw a Plymouth 'Hori-ZOHN' and we just laughed all night.❞

Adam also appeared as Opera Man, who sang news stories in a made-up foreign language. To understand the nonsense noises Adam was making, viewers had to read subtitles. One of his best-known verses is:

❝Brad Pitt sexiest, *People* wrote-oh, Operaman say, Recount the vote-oh!❞

The lyrics he sang were made funnier by a picture of *People* magazine that appeared on the screen behind Adam with the caption "Operaman: Sexiest Man Alive."

One of the joys of being on *SNL* for Adam was the chance to work with interesting people like fellow comedians David Spade, Chris Rock, and Chris Farley. They became friends as well as coworkers and continually tried to push each other to be funnier. Spade thinks Adam is a very funny person. This is how Spade tried to describe Adam's humor for *People* magazine:

❝Adam's kind of the Everyman. You feel smarter than him. You feel sorry for him. And call it dim wit

Adam Sandler sings about his red sweatshirt with Kevin Nealon during the regular Weekend Update segment of *Saturday Night Live,* **broadcast in February 1993. Adam was known not only for singing silly songs on the show but also for creating a variety of memorable characters with names like Opera Man, Canteen Boy, and Cajun Man.**

or dumb luck, you just can't help wanting to watch him. It's a different kind of funny. It's like smart, thought-out dumb. **"**

Adam's love of music led him to apply his unique brand of comedy to writing funny songs. The most memorable was "The Chanukah Song," a humorous tune about the Jewish holiday. Adam first sang the song on *Saturday Night Live* in 1994, and it was immediately popular. It became an even bigger hit two years later, when Adam transferred it to a new segment of his career—recording comedy albums.

CROSS-CURRENTS

If you'd like to find out more about one of Adam's most popular comedy songs, read "The Chanukah Song." Go to page 52. ▶▶

A September 1992 photo of the cast of *Saturday Night Live*. From left, front row, are Chris Farley, Al Franken, and Melanie Hutsell. In the middle row, from left, are Chris Rock, Julia Sweeney, Dana Carvey, and Rob Schneider. In the back row, from left, are Adam Sandler, David Spade, Ellen Cleghorne, Kevin Nealon, Phil Hartman, and Tim Meadows.

⫸ THE RECORDING STAR ⫷

The fame Adam got from being funny on *SNL* made it possible for him to start making comedy albums. His first album was *They're All Gonna Laugh at You!* Since the album was released in 1993, people have bought more than 3 million copies. His second album—*What the Hell Happened to Me?*—came out in 1996 and was also a big success.

Adam's fans bought his albums even though the jokes, skits, and songs he performed were darker and more off-color than the brand of humor he was allowed to do on television. The dialogue on the albums was also laced with obscenities, but his fans did not seem to mind the swear words because they still thought he was funny. The first album included a skit called "Assistant-Principal's-Big-Day" in which the assistant principal gets to run the school when the principal is sick. The routine is sexually explicit as it describes the new principal taking advantage of his new role.

Not all of Adam's comedy humor was offensive. One song, "Lunchlady Land," was about a woman who serves meals to students. He

When Adam recorded his first album, *They're All Gonna Laugh at You*, he was in the middle of his five-season career at *Saturday Night Live*. The album, released in September 1993, also featured *SNL* performers Rob Schneider, David Spade, and Tim Meadows and SNL writer Conan O'Brien. The album earned Adam a Grammy nomination.

later said that the song had been inspired by a woman who had served meals at Hayden Hall when he was attending New York University.

Adam's 1999 release *Stan and Judy's Kid* set a record for most comedy albums sold in the first week it was available for purchase. Overall, Adam has sold more than 4.5 million copies of his five comedy albums. With that kind of success, people are surprised he has not made more comedy albums. The reason is that he has been too busy making movies.

ADAM BECOMES A MOVIE STAR

One reason Adam had desperately wanted to get a job with *Saturday Night Live* was that many of the show's performers had been able to make the jump from television to making movies. Before *SNL*, Adam's only movie appearance had been a bit part in *Going Overboard* in 1989, a film that came out as a video and was never shown in theaters. But his growing fame from television helped him get a few more parts in pictures, including *Coneheads*, a 1993 movie based on an *SNL* skit featuring aliens with cone-shaped heads visiting Earth. The movie starred Dan Aykroyd and Jane Curtin and featured other comedy stars like David Spade, Drew Carey, Ellen DeGeneres, and Jon Lovitz.

The movies, however, did not showcase Adam's own unique brand of humor. Adam believed that the type of jokes he told and the characters he created were funny. However, his comedy was very different from mainstream comedy. He knew that movies other people wrote would not reflect his offbeat style of humor. So he and NYU roommate Tim Herlihy wrote a script about a spoiled rich young man whose father makes him repeat school from kindergarten through high school. After several studios rejected the idea for the movie, Universal Studios finally agreed to make it. The movie was *Billy Madison*.

A starring role in a movie he helped write was a big step forward for Adam. He was nervous about how people would react to the film because he knew it could make him famous as a film star and not just as a television or nightclub comic. The fact that he had helped write the script for the movie put even more pressure on him. Just before the movie came out in February 1995, he told *Entertainment Weekly*:

> **❝Billy's the closest I've come to playing myself. I feel so much pressure because I want it to be as**

A scene from the 1995 film *Billy Madison*. In Sandler's first commercially successful hit, which he cowrote, he stars as Billy, the heir to the Madison Hotel fortune. But since Billy has been irresponsible for most of his life, he has to prove to his father that he deserves the inheritance by repeating 12 grades of school in six months.

good as it can be. [Comedian] Dennis Miller told me that you only get famous once and then you are famous. But the best part is becoming famous. Right now I'm the underdog. It feels good. **"**

The movie was not a big hit, but Adam was good enough to earn a nomination for an MTV Movie Award for Best Comedic Performance. Although Adam did not win, he knew he would be able to get more movie roles. As a result, Adam quit *Saturday Night Live* after having been a star on the show for five years. His future now would be in movies, not television.

Summer's Best Movie Posters

Entertainment WEEKLY

...NKS in Stephen King's GREEN MILE

#490 · June 18, 199...

HOW THE STAR OF **BIG DADDY** BECAME THE MOST BANKABLE DOOFUS IN HOLLYWOOD

REVENGE OF THE NERD

ADAM SANDLER

Adam Sandler on the June 18, 1999, cover of *Entertainment Weekly*. After leaving *Saturday Night Live* in 1995, the comedian focused on making movies, typically starring as a lovable goof who somehow manages to get the girl. In addition to making box-office hits, Adam also appeared frequently on popular TV talk shows.

4

Movie Mogul

ADAM TOOK A RISK WHEN HE QUIT *SATURDAY Night Live* (*SNL*). Many actors who have starred on television have failed in the movie industry. Despite his talent and television fame, Adam's new career started slowly. His first few films, *Billy Madison* (1995), *Happy Gilmore* (1996), and *Bulletproof* (1996), did not make a lot of money.

In addition, most movie critics did not like Adam's movies. For example, in his review of *Happy Gilmore*, a comedy about an out-of-control hockey player who becomes a professional golfer, *People* magazine's Tom Gliatto told readers not to bother seeing the movie. He claimed that he could not understand why Adam's fans liked him. Adam's fans, however, flocked to the movie despite the bad reviews.

One of the movie's scenes has become a film classic. In the movie, Gilmore starts arguing with famed game-show host Bob Barker while they are playing golf during a **pro-am** event. Eventually the two become so mad at each other that they start fighting. The fight is funny because the senior citizen eventually beats up Adam's character. (Barker had said he would not make the **cameo** appearance in the movie unless he won the fight, even though he was 82 years old.) Newspaper and magazine reviewers ridiculed the fight, but it was good enough to win an MTV Movie Award for Best Fight because so many people loved it.

⇒ DISLIKED BY CRITICS ⇐

In 1998, Adam finally hit the big time. His film *The Wedding Singer*, a romantic comedy that costarred Drew Barrymore, earned more than $80 million at the **box office**. Later that year *The Waterboy*, a comedy about a goofy young man from Louisiana who becomes a college football star, became an even bigger hit. During the first three days it was in theaters in November 1998, his fans bought tickets totaling $39.4 million. The box-office bonanza was a record for a non-summer movie opening. Overall, *The Waterboy* earned more than $160 million.

These successes proved that in just a few years Adam Sandler had become one of the world's most popular movie stars. But even though millions of fans loved Adam, most movie critics did not like his performances. Bobby Boucher, the character Adam created in *The Waterboy*, is juvenile, acts like an idiot, and talks in a whiny voice better suited for a dim-witted 12-year-old. Film reviewers like Roger Ebert complained about Adam's work.

Adam's success at getting people to go to movies that reviewers do not like shows that he understands what average people want to watch. Lorne Michaels, who had hired Adam for *SNL*, has said that critics use the wrong set of values to judge Adam's early movies:

> **"**It's unfair to put Adam's comedies into the larger world of film. It is like comparing candy to the whole world of food. Everyone knows what a Snickers is and why you like it. To deconstruct it, to point out that it only has peanuts and chocolate, is to take all the fun out of eating it. **"**

Negative reviews did not upset Adam very much. He has said that the only critics who matter are the people who watch him, whether in a

In the 1998 romantic comedy *The Wedding Singer*, Adam plays a former high school musician who sings cover songs at weddings. When his fiancée leaves him, he has a breakdown. But then Julia, played by Drew Barrymore, asks him to help with planning her own wedding, and the two begin to fall in love with each other.

nightclub, on television, or in a movie. He once told a Canadian newspaper reporter that a bad review could not shake his belief that he is humorous:

❝I know in my heart that I've always worked hard and tried to make funny movies. And I believe in my

movies, and critically I know a lot of critics object to what I do. But it can't hurt me that much. **99**

⇶ A MOVIE MOGUL ⇷

Because his style of humor was so unique, Adam knew it would be hard to find movies in which he could effectively use his comic talents. Adam had already written scripts for two of his own movies

Adam played simple-minded and good-natured Bobby Boucher, who carries water for the members of the university football team in the 1998 film *The Waterboy*. In this scene from the movie, the football coach, played by Henry Winkler, gives advice to Bobby, who will soon realize he has some athletic abilities to offer the team as well.

to better showcase his humor, *Billy Madison* and *Happy Gilmore.* In 1998 Adam decided to form a company so that he could make the kind of movies he liked. He named it Happy Madison Productions after two of his early movies.

As a movie producer, Adam would have even more control over his movies. A producer thinks up ideas for movies; writes or edits scripts; hires actors, directors, and other workers; and sometimes finances a film. To help with the workload, Adam hired friends from his college days or from his years at *Saturday Night Live,* because he liked them and respected their talent. They have been nicknamed Team Sandler.

The first movie Adam's company produced was *Deuce Bigalow: Male Gigolo.* The 1999 film starred another former *Saturday Night Live* star, Rob Schneider. The following year Happy Madison produced *Little Nicky,* a film in which Adam starred as the son of the devil.

CROSS-CURRENTS

For more information about the many friends who have helped Adam Sandler succeed as a movie producer, check out "Team Sandler." Go to page 52. ▶▶

⇛ COMEDIES AND EVEN DRAMAS! ⇚

His box-office clout gave Adam the chance to make many different types of movies. Many were comedies, such as *Big Daddy.* This 1999 film was about a carefree young man who unexpectedly has to take care of a five-year-old boy for a few days. It was another huge hit, earning more than $160 million, and featured the manic comedy that had made Adam famous.

The **plot** of the 2002 film *Mr. Deeds* centered on how a nice person reacts to becoming instantly rich and famous after inheriting $40 billion. As he had in *The Wedding Singer,* Adam toned down his hyper-silliness to make his character more believable. The film was still funny, but one reviewer wrote that it was perhaps the first time an Adam Sandler movie could be called mild instead of wild.

Around this same time, Adam began making more **comedy dramas**. In 2002 he starred in *Punch-Drunk Love* with Emily Watson. The film was about a social misfit with a fiery temper who manages to overcome his problems and find true love. Adam received good reviews for his dramatic acting in the movie, and that led him to make more films that were not strictly comedies.

ADAM SANDLER

Adam was nominated for an MTV Award for Best Comedic Performance for his role in the 2002 film *Mr. Deeds*. He starred as Longfellow Deeds, a small-town nobody who inherits a $40 billion media empire from a distant relative. Peter Gallagher (center) and Erick Avari (left) appear as the deceased tycoon's partners who try to cheat Longfellow out of his inheritance.

⋙ *ANGER MANAGEMENT* ⋘

For the 2003 film *Anger Management*, Adam teamed up with Jack Nicholson, one of the greatest actors in film history. Nicholson played a rude therapist who tries, with hilarious results, to help

Adam's movie character tame his anger. At first, a lot of people thought that pairing Nicholson, a celebrated dramatic actor, with Adam, who is known for his nutty humor, would be a big mistake. Even Nicholson was not sure if he wanted to make the movie at first. But the unusual pairing worked, and the movie earned more than $133 million.

CROSS-CURRENTS

To find out why Jack Nicholson agreed to star in Anger Management, read "Jack Nicholson Is a Risk Taker." Go to page 53. ▶▶

One of Adam's best-reviewed films was the 2002 dramatic comedy *Punch-Drunk Love*. In the film, he starred as a quiet, socially awkward man who is transformed when a beautiful woman, played by Emily Watson, enters his life. His performance in *Punch-Drunk Love* earned Sandler a Golden Globe nomination.

Adam Sandler and Jack Nicholson go head-to-head in this movie poster from the 2003 film *Anger Management*. Adam plays a mild-mannered man, Dave Buznik, who is ordered by the court to undergo anger management therapy at the hands of Nicholson, who plays specialist Dr. Buddy Rydell, a wild-eyed and unpredictable psychotherapist.

Later, Nicholson said that when he had first met with Adam to discuss the movie, he had been impressed with how serious the comedian was, despite his weird sense of humor. Nicholson also discovered that he liked Adam. While Nicholson was filming *Anger Management*, he also discovered how popular Adam Sandler really was. Nicholson said when his own children visited the movie set, they spent more time with Adam than they did with him because they liked Adam's films so much. According to Nicholson:

> **My kids are crazy about Adam Sandler. He's like the Pied Piper! I was pretty impressed by it actually. They are literally mad for this man! We're shooting at MGM [Metro-Goldwyn-Mayer Studios], my kids come down and they're over with Adam.**

Because Adam's company was producing the film, Nicholson was actually working for the younger actor. He did not mind because Adam worked hard not only acting in the movie but doing other things to make the film successful. David Dorfman, who wrote the script for the film, had a similar experience working on the movie. Afterward, the writer described Adam as "a benevolent **mogul**." He said the film was a success because Adam worked so hard making script changes, helping edit film, and performing other tasks in addition to acting in the movie.

➢ GROWING UP PERSONALLY ⟵

While Adam was drawing praise for his professional career, he was also changing and growing personally. For years, he had been well known for playing jokes on people. For example, Adam liked calling friends and pretending to be someone else by disguising his voice. But in 1999 he told a reporter from England that he was trying to act more like an adult:

> **I'm trying to grow up. I want to grow up. I have a girlfriend. She wants me to grow up, I hear that 10 to 15 times a day (from her). I'm 32 and I think I'm starting to act like maybe I'm 15. I think next year I'll behave like I'm 18 and maybe one day I'll catch up with myself.**

ADAM SANDLER

His girlfriend was Jacqueline Samantha "Jackie" Titone, a model and actress he had met in 1998. Before they started dating, Adam had dated several women and at one time was engaged to Margaret Ruden, a manager of a cosmetics company. But after he met Titone, he stopped going out with anyone else. She even became a part of his professional life, as he made her a part of Team Sandler and gave her small parts in movies like *Big Daddy*.

Sandler's pet dog Meatball played a major role in the Jewish wedding ceremony uniting Adam Sandler and longtime girlfriend Jackie Titone on June 22, 2003. Both groom and dog sported a tux and a yarmulke—the traditional skullcap worn by Jewish men for religious reasons. Meatball carried the wedding band down the aisle on his back.

In 2002, Adam proposed to Titone during a day off from filming *Anger Management*. They were married in Malibu, California, on June 22, 2003. The wedding at an oceanfront mansion was attended by a host of big stars, including Jack Nicholson, Winona Ryder, Sharon Osbourne, Dustin Hoffman, and Quentin Tarantino.

The couple was married in a Jewish ceremony. Adam wore a tuxedo and a **yarmulke**. He also dressed his bulldog, Meatball, in a tuxedo and yarmulke because his pet was part of the wedding ceremony—the dog carried the wedding rings down the aisle on his back.

⇒ A REALLY BIG STAR ⇐

Adam's success made him one of the nation's most famous actors. In June 2003 he enjoyed a benefit of that fame by being invited back to Manchester Central High School as the guest speaker for the school's graduation ceremony. One reason Adam accepted was because his nephew was one of three class valedictorians graduating that year. It was also delightful for Adam to return triumphantly to the school where he had once been looked down on as a nutty, annoying class clown.

Adam Sandler leaves his footprints at Grauman's Chinese Theater in Hollywood, California, during a ceremony held on May 17, 2005. The honor of leaving an impression in the theater's cement courtyard has been granted to only about 200 personalities in the entertainment industry since Grauman's opened in 1927. Today, Hollywood considers Adam to be one of its superstars.

5

Adam Sandler, Superstar

MANY VETERAN ACTORS HAVE SAID THEY ENJOY working with Adam Sandler. One is Henry Winkler, who first became famous as Fonzie on the 1970s television show *Happy Days*. Winkler, who has appeared in several films with Sandler, says that Adam makes good films because he knows what is funnier better than anyone else:

> **❝**He's in charge of every detail of his comedy. He hears it in his head and guides whatever scene in the movie, whether he is in it or not, to his vision.**❞**

⇒ HITS AND MISSES ⇐

In 2004 Adam reunited with Drew Barrymore for *50 First Dates*, a romantic comedy about a man who falls in love with a woman

ADAM SANDLER

who has short-term memory loss. After a car accident, Barrymore's character Lucy cannot remember anything about what had happened the previous day. This means that each day Adam's character, Henry, must reintroduce himself. The film was a big hit, earning more than $120 million, and many reviewers liked the movie.

Drew Barrymore and Adam Sandler at the 2004 premiere of *50 First Dates*, in Los Angeles, California. The romantic comedy, in which he and Barrymore paired up for the first time since *The Wedding Singer*, proved to be another box-office smash. In the film, he falls in love with a woman with short-term memory loss.

A second film that year was not as financially successful. *Spanglish* is about a wealthy American family, their Mexican housekeeper Flor, and Flor's daughter Cristina. The movie was a box-office flop, making just $55 million—less than the $80 million it had cost to make.

Adam bounced back from that film disappointment with *The Longest Yard* (2005), a remake of a 1975 hit about a prison football team that plays a game against prison guards. The movie is hilarious, but also has moments of dramatic intensity as Adam's character, Paul Crewe, learns some bitter lessons about himself. The film earned nearly $160 million. Some people went to the movie because they liked football or other actors in the movie, such as Burt Reynolds and Chris Rock, but many of them walked out of theaters as new fans of Adam.

The next year, Adam had another hit with the comedy *Click*, about an overworked architect who learns a hard lesson about the importance of family time. The movie, which also starred Kate Beckinsale and Christopher Walken, made over $70 million.

➤ ADAM'S MOST DIFFICULT ROLE ◄

Although Adam's earliest movies were simple comedies that made people laugh, films like *Spanglish* and *Click* made moviegoers think about their lives. These films tested Adam's ability to create complex characters. One of his biggest acting challenges to date came in 2007's *Reign Over Me*. That film showed that Adam had become a fine actor as well as a box-office star.

In *Reign Over Me* Adam plays Charlie Fineman, whose wife and two daughters were among the nearly 3,000 people killed in the September 11, 2001, terrorist attack on New York. Fineman has so much trouble dealing with the loss of his family that he retreats from reality. He wanders around New York like a crazy person, sometimes using a scooter as his means of transportation. Adam's character regains his sanity through the help of Alan Johnson, an old friend played by Don Cheadle. The two had attended college together but had not seen each other in many years. When they meet early in the movie, Cheadle is heartbroken to discover what has happened to his old friend. He decides to try to help Fineman recover from his grief and have a normal life again. In the process of helping Fineman, Cheadle's character learns a lot about himself and how he needs to change to be a better, happier person. The movie is as much about

CROSS-CURRENTS

To find out how Mike Binder came up with the concept for his film, read "The Idea for Reign Over Me." Go to page 54. ▶▶

the power of friendship as it is about how a survivor of that terrible day finally regains the ability to go on with his life.

When director Mike Binder offered Sandler the part, Adam was not sure at first whether he could play such an intense, dramatic role. Adam knew he was still known mainly as a comedian, and a crazy one at that. He liked the story so much that he told Binder he should find another actor for the movie who was more suited to such a difficult role. But the story fascinated Adam so much that he finally agreed to do the film.

Adam works hard to create his film characters, even the goofy ones who just seem to act silly. To make Fineman real, Adam went to therapy sessions with **9-11** survivors. He told the *San Francisco Chronicle* how he researched his role:

> **❝**I met with a lot of people who lost their family in 9/11 and other disasters. I sat with them in therapy and talked to them outside of there. They told me a lot about their lives and how they handled it day to day—what they're afraid of and what they're scared to do.**❞**

⟫ GOOD REVIEWS ⟪

Adam combined what he learned from those sessions with his acting skills to make Fineman seem like a real person to moviegoers. His performance was so good that movie critics who usually attacked him showered him with praise. One reviewer wrote:

> **❝**Adam Sandler proved that he could really act rather than just play the same dunderheaded goofball that made him famous.**❞**

Adam's next movie was the laugh-filled *I Now Pronounce You Chuck and Larry*. It proved once again that Adam was still a box-office champion as one of the funniest people making movies. *Reign Over Me*, however, had shown the world how Adam's acting abilities had matured over the years. Not surprisingly, Adam had also matured as a person.

In the 2007 film *Reign Over Me* Adam stars as Charlie Fineman, a man who withdraws from life after losing his wife and children to the terrorist attacks of September 11 in New York. Eventually, with the help of a friend, he begins to come back to life. The movie, as well as Sandler's dramatic performance, received many positive reviews.

⋙ ADAM BECOMES A DAD ⋘

Despite his juvenile humor that somehow found its way into every part of his life, Adam was trying to act more responsible as he grew older. And he did not have to look far to find role models for the responsible adult he wanted to become—his dad and his older brother, Scott. Adam had always loved and admired his father, who he has said was his best friend while he was growing up. Before he had even begun to think about getting married and having children, he had known that he wanted to treat his own children with as much love and affection as his father had shown him.

Adam was also close to Scott when they were children, and that relationship had continued into adulthood. Even though Adam was a big movie star, he once told a reporter that he felt his brother was the one who was the real hero in the family. Adam believed that because he knew that his brother was a good father to his two children. In a 2004 interview with Rebecca Murray, Adam said he admired his brother's loving way as a father:

> **❝That's how I got to grow up and that's how I plan on raising my kids. ❞**

Being a good parent is a true test of whether someone is a responsible adult. Adam finally got his chance to become that loving father on May 5, 2006, when his daughter, Sadie Madison, was born. He had an opportunity to think about what fatherhood means because that same year he had starred in *Click*. In that film, Adam's architect character Michael Newman learns that he needs to be a good husband and father to be truly happy. Adam told journalist Paul Fischer that the movie made him think about his own life:

> **❝Looking back on the past 10 years of my life I've been at work more than I've been at home, so I connected with this movie. By the end of the movie, when I watched the playback the other day, I was excited to get home and do the right thing—be with the family. ❞**

For Adam, that meant lavishing love on his wife Jackie and his newborn daughter Sadie. And just as his character in *Big Daddy*

Adam and Jackie Sandler, along with daughter Sadie Madison, attend a fundraiser for the EB Medical Research Foundation, which provides support for research on the treatment of a rare genetic disorder called epidermolysis bullosa (EB). The Kinerase Skincare CelEBration on the Pier, was held on September 29, 2007, in Santa Monica, California.

truly enjoyed children, Adam is having a ball being a father. When Sadie was just a month old, Adam told *People* magazine:

> **"The baby situation is fine. I love that kid. Every day I get more and more excited, and I feel comfortable with her."**

CROSS-CURRENTS

To learn more about Adam Sandler's charitable work, check out "Adam Sandler Likes to Help People." Go to page 55. ▶▶

⋙ ADAM STILL LOVES HIS WORK ⋘

Adam's love for his family, however, has not kept him from his other love—making people laugh. In early 2008 Adam was putting the finishing touches on two more movies that were expected to be box-office hits.

Bedtime Stories is a family comedy about a man whose life changes when the imaginative bedtime stories he tells his nephews start to magically come true. The movie marks Adam's first film for Disney Studios. *You Don't Mess with the Zohan* has a typically strange plot for a Sandler movie. Adam plays the title character,

When he can take the time off from work and family, Adam may be found in a wetsuit, surfing in the Pacific waters near his beach house, which is in Malibu, California. A longtime fan of surfing, Adam has even sung about it. "Pibb Goes Surfing" appears in Sandler's 2004 album *Shhh, Don't Tell*.

Zohan, a former secret agent for Israel who fakes his death so he can move to New York City and become a hair stylist. In addition to starring in the movie with Emmanuelle Chriqui and friends Rob Schneider and Henry Winkler, Adam helped write the script and Happy Madison Productions produced the film.

Family responsibilities haven't stopped Adam from continuing to entertain millions of people. But balancing his personal and professional lives can be hard. Even big stars like Adam can face difficult times. For example, Adam was devastated in 2003 by the death of his dad, whom he loved very much. A few years later, Adam relived that grief when he played the role of Michael Newman in *Click*. In one scene, Newman uses a magical remote control to review his life, and he fast-forwards through the painful death of his father.

In a 2006 interview, Adam admitted that his life is not always perfect. He also said that when bad things happen, he does his best to handle them because he knows things will always get better:

> **" There are things that get you bummed, but I enjoy my life, and don't want to fast-forward it. Some parts are boring, some parts are tired, but it goes away and you get back to having good times. "**

It sounds strange to have someone who has played so many strange characters deliver such sound, practical advice on living. But unlike the roles he plays, Adam Sandler is a very intelligent, likable person. It is only in the movies that the nice guy pretends to be a weirdo.

Buddies in Real Life

Actor Kevin James may have enjoyed making *I Now Pronounce You Chuck and Larry* as much as people who went to see the hit comedy enjoyed watching the movie. That is because he and Adam Sandler became good friends and had a lot of fun making the film. In an interview with *USA Today* newspaper, Kevin said:

"Adam treats everyone on the cast incredibly—all his friends and people he has been working with for years. . . . He takes care of his friends and family. Adam wants to help everybody out and have a good time."

When the actors were not working on scenes during long 14-hour days of filming, they joked around with each other and watched movies. It was easy for them to become friends because they had followed similar career paths to stardom. Both of them had started working as stand-up comics in nightclubs, then gained fame in television, and were now concentrating on making movies.

Adam and Kevin also bonded because of their passion for baseball, even though they like different New York teams. Adam roots for the Yankees, while Kevin is a rabid Mets fan. They went with each other to games of both their favorite teams. (Go back to page 6.) ◀◀

Adam Sandler (left) and Kevin James in a scene from I Now Pronounce You Chuck and Larry. *In an e-mail sent to a reporter, Adam once wrote, "Me and Kevin are remarkably similar. We both come from incredibly nice New York families. We both have beautiful families of our own. And we are both huge Adam Sandler fans."*

A Loving Family

Adam has explored the role and responsibilities of fatherhood in his movies Spanglish, Click, *and* Reign Over Me. *However, when talking about how he wants to be a father to his own daughter, Adam looks to his father. In a song that he dedicated to Stan Sandler, Adam says his dad "was my hero—the coolest guy ever, I swear."*

Adam Sandler is grateful for the loving way his parents raised him, and has occasionally spoken about his life growing up. In a 2004 interview, Adam told journalist Jeff Otto:

"The thing that I always think about with my parents is when my parents would get a phone call, 'Hey, we're going away to Bermuda this weekend. You want to come? But, we're not bringing the kids.' My parents would go, 'No kids? Oh no, then we can't go.' That was my father and mother's sacrifice. They didn't care about anything but the kids. I never had a speech from my father [saying], 'This is what you must do or shouldn't do' but I just learned to be led by example. My father wasn't perfect. He had a temper. I took some of that. He would snap, but the older he got, he started calming down. He learned about life, but the thing that he taught my whole family was that family was the most important thing and, no matter what, if a family member needs you, you go and help them out, you get there. He just made us feel comfortable and respectful to other families, my mother also."

(Go back to page 12.)

Jewish Comedians

Adam Sandler is a funny guy who is proud of his Jewish heritage. There have been many talented and successful Jewish comedians. Many of the comedians who influenced Adam while he was growing up were Jewish, like the Marx Brothers. Other Jewish comedians who starred in movies and television include Milton Berle, Sid Caesar, Woody Allen, Mel Brooks, and Jerry Seinfeld, who had one of the most popular shows in television history.

In *The Haunted Smile: The Story of Jewish Comedians in America*, author Lawrence Epstein explains that many Jewish people developed a sense of humor to cope with bad things that happened to them. Many Jewish immigrants to the United States in the 20th century suffered from either poverty or religious discrimination.

Although Adam's family was comfortable financially, he has admitted that some students in Manchester rejected him because he was Jewish. He also heard anti-Jewish comments on the school bus. In an interview with *Mademoiselle* magazine, Adam explains:

❝I was always a little bit of an outcast. Everywhere I went, I heard comments about being Jewish. And it would hurt.❞

In 1989 writer and comedian Jerry Seinfeld brought his stand-up comedy to the television screen with a highly popular sitcom called Seinfeld. *Although the program ended in 1998, it continues to be broadcast today through syndication. Meanwhile, Jerry Seinfeld continues to entertain the public by performing on the comedy club circuit.*

Instead of fighting kids who acted in a prejudiced way, Adam used humor to defuse the tense situation and win his tormentors over as friends.

(Go back to page 14.)

The Power of *Saturday Night Live*

Saturday Night Live debuted on October 11, 1975. The late-night 90-minute show broadcast from New York features comedy skits and music and is one of the few television shows that is aired live. Adam Sandler was only nine years old when *SNL* started, but he quickly became a fan of the show because it featured the nation's funniest young comedians. He grew to love original cast members like Dan Aykroyd, John Belushi, and Chevy Chase. The comedy they and their successors on the show performed appealed to Adam because it was fresh, original, and often outlandish.

Because of *SNL*'s popularity, its cast members soon became famous enough to begin making movies. One of the first was *The Blues Brothers*, a 1980 film that expanded on characters that Aykroyd and Belushi had developed on *SNL*: "Joliet" Jake and Elwood Blues, two crazy brothers wearing dark suits and dark glasses who love blues music. They were only the first of many *SNL* regulars who would vault to movie stardom. Other former *Saturday Night Live* cast members who have become movie stars include Chevy Chase, Bill Murray, Eddie Murphy, Billy Crystal, Martin Short, Dana Carvey, Mike Myers, Will Ferrell, and Tina Fey. (Go back to page 20.) ◀◀

Former Saturday Night Live *cast members Chris Kattan (left) and Will Ferrell. After leaving SNL in 2006, Kattan went on to star in the films* Undercover Brother *(2002) and* Adam & Steve *(2005). Will Ferrell, who left SNL in 2002 has appeared in* Old School *(2003),* Elf *(2003),* The Producers *(2006) and* Stranger than Fiction *(2007), among many others.*

"The Chanukah Song"

Adam Sandler's "Chanukah Song" mentions the names of a number of well-known men and women who most people may not realize are Jewish, such as actors Paul Newman and Goldie Hawn, rock star David Lee Roth, and Hall of Fame baseball player Rod Carew. Adam first performed the humorous tune on *Saturday Night Live* in 1994. The song gained new popularity when he included it on his 1996 comedy album *What the Hell Happened to Me?*

Adam wrote the song to be funny, but it has made many Jewish people proud. In 2002 Rabbi Irwin Kula of New York tried to explain why the silly song meant so much to Jewish people. Kula said that Jews have been discriminated against for so long that, at one time, some Jews were not comfortable with having their religious and ethnic background made public. Kula explained that the fact that it is now all right for people to be known as Jewish marks an important step in their acceptance by U.S. society. The rabbi said:

"It's funny, and it's normal. . . . This is a remarkable moment in Jewish history, and American history. There's no way that song could have been performed 40 years ago."

(Go back to page 21.)

Team Sandler

The people who work for Adam Sandler at Happy Madison Productions have been nicknamed Team Sandler because they work together as a team to make movies. They could also be called "Friends of Sandler" because so many of them are his old friends.

Tim Herlihy, his roommate at New York University (NYU), helped Adam write many of his most successful movies. The NYU connection also includes Frank Coraci, who has directed Sandler hits like *The Wedding Singer*, and Jack Giarraputo, who helps Adam with the business end of producing movies. Adam has also cast NYU roommate Allen Covert in several movies, including *50 First Dates*.

Adam likes to use his old pals in film projects because he trusts them personally and professionally. He also does that because he is the kind of person who is loyal to his old friends. That same spirit of friendship has also led Adam to hire many performers he worked with on *Saturday Night Live* for the films his company makes. *SNL* buddies that have worked in movies with Adam include Dana Carvey, Norm Macdonald, Kevin Nealon, Colin Quinn, Rob Schneider, and David Spade.

(Go back to page 31.)

Jack Nicholson Is a Risk Taker

In 2003 many people were surprised when Jack Nicholson agreed to star with Adam Sandler in *Anger Management* because Nicholson is best known for serious dramatic roles. He has won three **Academy Awards** and has starred in many great films, such as *Terms of Endearment*, *Chinatown*, *One Flew over the Cuckoo's Nest*, and *The Shining*. Nicholson had never acted in the kind of slapstick comedies for which Adam was famous. But Nicholson told journalist Robin Walker that he relished the challenge of trying something new:

"I think it's the extreme things in life that make good cinema. Every character is different, that's what makes it interesting. Otherwise I wouldn't keep doing it. This is kind of antic comedy, as opposed to dark, wry comedy, so working with Adam in this picture, in a way, defies my own conventions. Every once in a while you have to do this otherwise you begin to settle in. Sometimes when you have success it traps you and I think this is something specific to the movie business. You don't even know it until you're in it. As an actor you have to keep growing, it's part of the craft.**"**

(Go back to page 33.) ◀◀

On May 17, 2005, renowned actor Jack Nicholson (right) helped celebrate Adam Sandler's handprint and footprint ceremony at Grauman's Chinese Theater, on Hollywood Boulevard, in Los Angeles, California. Several decades earlier—on June 17, 1974—Nicholson had left his own concrete impressions at the Hollywood landmark.

The Idea for *Reign Over Me*

The September 11, 2001, terrorist attack on New York City was the most terrible act of aggression against U.S. civilians in the nation's history. Terrorists **hijacked** two airplanes and flew them into the World Trade Center, a giant commercial building in New York. The force of the crashes caused the building to collapse, killing nearly 3,000 people working there as well as emergency personnel trying to rescue them.

Mike Binder was in New York that day and witnessed the aftermath of the destruction. Binder, like most Americans, was deeply affected by the senseless act of violence. He was curious about what happened to the friends and relatives of the people killed that day. He wrote the script for *Reign Over Me* and directed the film. In an interview with a *Denver Post* reporter, Binder explains how he got the idea for the movie's plot:

The remains of the World Trade Center after the September 11, 2001, terrorist attacks. One reviewer praised the Mike Binder's story and the film based on the tragedy: "The incredibly moving post-9/11 drama Reign Over Me *proves that behind the funny guy facades of former stand-up comedians Mike Binder and Adam Sandler are a pair of very serious talents."*

❝I looked up and saw the towers burning. Later that night I was wandering and I saw a woman in Bryant Park crying her eyes out. You knew. You knew that that woman had lost her son or her daughter or her husband. There was a guttural wail. I wondered 'Who is still left behind? Who didn't get out of that day, even though they survived that day?'❞

(Go back to page 42.)

Adam Sandler Likes to Help People

Adam Sandler's talent for making people laugh has made him rich and famous. Adam tries to help other people who are less fortunate than he is because he knows he has been blessed in his life. One way Adam has helped people is to contribute money to worthy causes. His biggest gift was $1 million to the Boys and Girls Club in his hometown of Manchester, New Hampshire. When Adam made the donation on October 25, 2007, he said he did it because of his fond memories of playing basketball and Ping-Pong at the club while growing up. The huge donation helped the club expand and allow more children to have fun. In 2006 Adam gave 400 Play-Stations—their total cost was $100,000—to Israeli children who were victims of the war between Israel and Lebanon.

Many of his **humanitarian** activities involve lending his presence as a star to charitable events. Adam was one of the performers when cable television channel VH1 put on a telethon called *America: A Tribute to Heroes* to benefit victims of the September 11, 2001, terrorist attacks on the United States. He also performed—in his character as Operaman—at The Concert for New York City, a benefit to help the city's police officers, firefighters, and other rescue workers.

In 2005, when Adam starred in *The Longest Yard*, he and other actors in the movie went to St. Louis for the film's premiere to raise money for bone-marrow transplants. The charitable event was staged by rap star Nelly, one of the actors in the movie. Nelly started raising money to find more donors for such operations because his sister, Jacqueline "Jackie" Donahue, had died because she could not have one. Adam has also performed in charitable events to raise money for Autism Speaks, a group that helps children with autism.

Some charity events he participates in are fun. Like the character he played in *Happy Gilmore*, Adam loves to play golf, and he enjoyed playing with Jack Nicholson and other entertainment stars in a celebrity event to raise money to preserve old films for the future. However, Adam Sandler is a private person and he performs much of his charity work anonymously. For example, not many people know he has helped fight muscular dystrophy because a cousin has the disease.

(Go back to page 45.)

1966   Adam Richard Sandler is born on September 9.

1972   The Sandler family moves to Manchester, New Hampshire.

1984   Adam graduates from high school.

At the age of 17, he performs a comedy routine for the first time at Stitches Comedy Club in Boston, Massachusetts.

In the fall, he begins attending New York University.

1989   Adam makes his movie debut in *Going Overboard*.

1990   On December 8, Adam appears for the first time on *Saturday Night Live*.

1991   Adam graduates from New York University.

He continues to work as a writer and cast member on *Saturday Night Live*.

1993   Sandler releases his first comedy album, *They're All Gonna Laugh at You!*

1995   Adam leaves *Saturday Night Live*.

He lands his first starring movie role, in *Billy Madison*.

1996   Adam's fame increases with the release of *Happy Gilmore*.

1998   The success of the movies *The Wedding Singer* and *The Waterboy* makes Adam a huge star.

He creates Happy Madison Productions.

2003   On June 22, he marries Jacqueline Titone.

2006   On May 5, Sadie Madison, Adam's first child, is born.

2007   In March, *I Now Pronounce You Chuck and Larry* generates $34.2 million in ticket sales in its first three days in theaters.

2008   Two new movies, *You Don't Mess with the Zohan* and *Bedtime Stories*, are released.

Comedy Albums

1993 *They're All Gonna Laugh at You!*
1996 *What the Hell Happened to Me?*
1997 *What's Your Name?*
1999 *Stan and Judy's Kid*
2004 *Shhh . . . Don't Tell*

Television Shows

1987–90 *Remote Control*, 1987–1990
1987–88 *The Cosby Show*, "The Locker Room,""Dance Mania,"
"The Prom," and "The Visit"
1991–95 *Saturday Night Live* (44 episodes)

Movies

1989 *Going Overboard* (film debut)
1992 *Shakes the Clown*
1993 *Coneheads*
1994 *Airheads*
Mixed Nuts
1995 *Billy Madison*
1996 *Happy Gilmore*
Bulletproof
1998 *The Wedding Singer*
The Waterboy
Dirty Work
1999 *Big Daddy*
Deuce Bigalow: Male Gigolo
2000 *Little Nicky*
2001 *The Animal*
2002 *Mr. Deeds*
Punch-Drunk Love
Eight Crazy Nights
The Hot Chick
2003 *Anger Management*
2004 *50 First Dates*
Spanglish
2005 *The Longest Yard*
Deuce Bigalow: European Gigolo

2006 *Click*
2007 *Reign Over Me*
I Now Pronounce You Chuck and Larry
2008 *You Don't Mess with the Zohan*
Bedtime Stories

Awards

1996 MTV Movie Award, Best Fight for *Happy Gilmore*; shared with Bob Barker.

1998 MTV Movie Award, Best Kiss for *The Wedding Singer*; shared with Drew Barrymore.

1999 Blockbuster Entertainment Award, Favorite Actor-Comedy for *The Waterboy* and *The Wedding Singer*

Kids' Choice Award, Favorite Movie Actor for *The Waterboy* and *The Wedding Singer*

MTV Movie Award, Best Comedic Performance for *The Waterboy*

2000 Blockbuster Entertainment Award, Favorite Actor-Comedy for *Big Daddy*

Kids' Choice Award, Favorite Movie Actor for *Big Daddy*

MTV Movie Award, Best Comedic Performance for *Big Daddy*

People's Choice Award, Favorite Motion Picture Star in a Comedy

2001 Teen Choice Award, Choice Comedian

2002 Gijón International Film Festival, Best Actor for *Punch-Drunk Love*

Teen Choice Award, Choice Comedian

2003 Kids' Choice Awards, Favorite Movie Actor for *Mr. Deeds* and Favorite Voice from an Animated Movie for *Eight Crazy Nights*

Teen Choice Award, Choice Movie Hissy Fit for *Anger Management*.

2004 Teen Choice Award, Choice Comedian

2005 Kids' Choice Award, Favorite Movie Actor for *50 First Dates*

People's Choice Award, Favorite On-Screen Chemistry for *50 First Dates*; shared with Drew Barrymore

Teen Choice Award, Choice Comedian

2006 People's Choice Award, Favorite Funny Male Star

Teen Choice Award, Choice Comedian

2007 Kids' Choice Award, Favorite Male Movie Star for *Click*

Guys Choice Award, Ultimate Guy's Guy

Books

Epstein, Dwayne. *Adam Sandler*. San Diego: Lucent Books, 2004.

Horn, Geoffrey M. *Adam Sandler*. Milwaukee: Gareth Stevens, 2005.

Salem, Jon. *Adam Sandler: Not Too Shabby*. New York: Scholastic, 1999.

Seidman, David. *Adam Sandler*. Philadelphia: Chelsea House, 2000.

Web Sites

http://adamsandler.jt.org
> The Adam Sandler Experience bills itself as the oldest fan Web site about Sandler. It contains news and information about his movies, television appearances, and music.

http://movies.about.com
> About.com Hollywood Movies has facts about Adam Sandler films and links to news stories and Web sites about Sandler.

http://www.adamsandler.com
> Adam Sandler's official Web site has articles, photographs, and videos, including personal messages to fans from Sandler.

http://www.imdb.com
> The Internet Movie Database has detailed information on all of Adam Sandler's television and movie appearances as well as pictures, news articles, and links to other sites about Sandler.

http://www.tvguide.com/celebrities/adam-sandler/138176
> This site contains a biography, news stories, pictures, and other Web site listings about Adam Sandler.

Publisher's note:
The Web sites mentioned in this book were active at the time of publication. The publisher is not responsible for Web sites that have changed their addresses or discontinued operation since the date of publication. The publisher will review and update the Web site addresses each time the book is reprinted.

Academy Awards—awards that the Academy of Motion Picture Arts and Sciences give to actors and others who create movies.

audition—a tryout for a film, TV, or stage role.

box office—the place where tickets to a movie or theatrical performance are sold.

cameo—a small part in a movie.

casting agent—someone who finds jobs for performers.

comedy dramas—movies that have elements of both funny and dramatic films.

episode—one of multiple shows in a television series.

heckle—to interrupt a performance or speech.

hijack—to illegally take control of an airplane by force.

humanitarian—someone who tries to help other people who are less fortunate.

improvisational—to instantly improvise or make up jokes to fit a situation.

mogul—a nickname for someone who is important in the film industry.

9-11—shorthand for the September 11, 2001, terrorist attacks on the United States.

plot—the story a movie tells.

pro-am—when professional golfers play with amateurs to raise money for charity.

producer—a person who is involved in the business end of making a movie.

script—the dialogue and actions for a play or movie.

skits—segments of a show in which one or more people tell jokes or perform humorous scenes.

stand-up comedian—a person who tells jokes or performs a skit in front of an audience.

yarmulke—a cloth head covering Jewish men wear for religious reasons.

page 6 "I've been called a moron . . . " Lesley O'Toole, "I'm a Millionaire Moron." *Independent Arts and Books Review* (September 22, 2006), p. 9.

page 9 "The most heavily dramatic Sandler . . ." William Arnold, "Sandler Scores with a Dramatic Turn in 'Reign.'" *Seattle Post-Intelligencer* (March 23, 2007), p. 7.

page 12 "He used our school . . . " Cheryl Westbrook, "Nease Principal Aided Future Comic Star Sandler." *Florida Times Union* (December 20, 2000), p. L1.

page 14 "It took a lot . . . " Mick LaSalle, "Why Adam's the Apple of Moviegoers' Eyes." *San Francisco Chronicle* (June 20, 1999), p. 32.

page 18 "I remember telling Hanks . . . " Tom Shales and James Andrew Miller, *Live from New York* (Boston: Little, Brown, 2002), p. 31.

page 20 "It's just a stupid thing . . . " Christopher Rose, "Cajunman Adds His Own Accent to SNL." *Times-Picayune* (April 21, 1992), p. C1.

page 20 "Brad Pitt sexiest, *People* wrote-oh . . . " *Saturday Night Live: The Best of Adam Sandler*, DVD (Santa Monica, CA: Lions Gate, November 9, 1999).

page 20 "Adam's kind of the Everyman . . . " "The 25 Most Intriguing People of '98: Adam Sandler." *People* (December 28, 1998), p. 97.

page 24 "Billy's the closest I've come . . . " Kate Meyers, "Adam Ribs." *Entertainment Weekly* (February 17, 1995), p. 26.

page 28 "It's unfair to put Adam's . . . " Richard Corliss, "Sandler Happens." *Time* (February 1, 1999), p. 59.

page 29 "I know in my heart . . . " Prairie Miller, "Adam Sandler: *Punch-Drunk Love* Interview." *Mini Movie Reviews* (October 14, 2002). http://www.minireviews.com/interviews/punch.html.

page 35 "My kids are crazy about . . . " Andy Dougan, "Angry . . . Who Me?" *Glasgow, Scotland, Evening Times* (June 5, 2003), p. 12.

page 35 "I'm trying to grow up . . . " Alison Jones, "Growing Up Fast: Adam Sandler, One of the Hottest Properties to Hit the Comedy Film Scene—and One of the Biggest Earning Stars—Talks to Alison Jones." *Birmingham, United Kingdom, Post* (October 2, 1999), p. 5.

page 39 "He's in charge of every . . . " Betty Cortina, "Stop the Presses." *Entertainment Weekly* (June 18, 1999), p. 24.

page 42 "I met with a lot . . . " Peter Hartlaub, "Hey, It's Adam Sandler! But What's This? A drama?" *San Francisco Chronicle* (March 21, 2007), p. E1.

page 42 "Adam Sandler proved that he . . . " L. Kent Wolgamott, "Adam Sandler Proved That He Is Right as 'Reign.'" *Lincoln Journal Star* (March 23, 2007), p. 4.

page 44 "That's how I got to . . . " Rebecca Murray, "Adam Sandler Talks About Playing a Dad Onscreen and Working with James L. Brooks" (December 1, 2004). http://movies.about.com/od/spanglish/a/spangas121004.html.

page 44 "Looking back on the past . . . " Paul Fischer, "Dark Horizons Interview: Adam Sandler for 'Click'" (June 12, 2006). http://www.darkhorizons.com/news06/click2.php.

page 45 "The baby situation is fine . . . " "More Proud Papas." *People* (June 12, 2006), p. 49.

page 47 "There are things that get . . . " "Enough About Me, Sandler Says; Being Ignored . . . That's the Life." *Concord Monitor* (June 19, 2006), p.C12.

page 48 "Adam treats everyone on the . . . " Donna Freydkin, "Kevin James Weds Humor with Sensibility." *USA Today* (July 19, 2007), p. 02d.

page 49 "The thing that I . . ." Jeff Otto, "Interview: Adam Sandler, IGN FilmForce Talks with the Often Shy Comic About Playing It More Serious in James L. Brooks' *Spanglish*" (December 15, 2004). http://movies.ign.com/articles/573/573716p1.html.

page 50 "I was always a little . . . " Meredith Berkman, "Adam Sandler Is a Very Funny Guy." *Mademoiselle* (March 1995), p. 98.

page 52 "It's funny, and it's normal . . . " Paul Farhi, "Sandler Keeps Hanukkah Spotlight on Jewish Celebs." *South Florida Sun-Sentinel* (December 13, 2002), p. 10E.

page 53 "I think it's the extreme . . . " Robin Walker, "Jack of All Trades." *Liverpool, England, Daily Post* (May 31, 2003), p. 2.

page 54 "I looked up and saw . . . " Lisa Kennedy, "Director Takes Actors' Cues in Brave 'Reign.'" *Denver Post* (March 23, 2007), p. F1.

Numbers in **bold italics** refer to captions.

Michael V. Uschan has written more than 60 books, including biographies of contemporary figures such as Tiger Woods and Tupac Shakur and historical figures such as U.S. presidents Abraham Lincoln and John F. Kennedy. Mr. Uschan began his career as a journalist, and considers writing history books a natural extension of the skills he developed during his many years in journalism. He and his wife, Barbara, reside in the Milwaukee suburb of Franklin, Wisconsin.

PICTURE CREDITS